FIRST EDITION

Writing after Midnight:
An Advanced Guide to Composition and Research

By Ernesto Rueda

cognella® | ACADEMIC PUBLISHING

Bassim Hamadeh, CEO and Publisher
Kassie Graves, Director of Acquisitions and Sales
Jamie Giganti, Senior Managing Editor
Miguel Macias, Senior Graphic Designer
Angela Schultz, Senior Field Acquisitions Editor
Michelle Piehl, Project Editor
Alexa Lucido, Licensing Coordinator
Abbey Hastings, Associate Production Editor
Joyce Lue, Interior Designer

Cover image copyright © 2012 iStockphoto LP/catnap72.
Copyright © 2013 iStockphoto LP/RedBarnStudio.
Copyright © 2013 iStockphoto LP/endopack.
Copyright © 2014 iStockphoto LP/ricardoreitmeyer.
Copyright © 2015 iStockphoto LP/shapecharge.
Copyright © 2016 iStockphoto LP/lechatnoir.

Printed in the United States of America

ISBN: 978-1-63487-933-0 (pbk) / 978-1-63487-934-7 (br)

CONTENTS

PREFACE

Perfecting research and argumentative writing requires attention to detail. You will find your voice in the process and be perceived as more academic and sophisticated, which is required in higher education and your profession.

The wheel is not being reinvented here. The basic format of an essay remains the same. An introduction, which features the thesis near the end of the paragraph, is where you begin. Supporting paragraphs follow, and the final paragraph will be the conclusion. For papers of considerable length (ten pages or more), it is reasonable to have a multi-paragraph introduction and conclusion.

Think of the format, guidelines, and rules as a blueprint or recipe. In order to construct a successful paper, you must follow the rules. You cannot ignore a blueprint or recipe and expect to get the desired result. Approach academic writing as a technical process. Meet the requirements of the assignment. Follow the blueprint. Provide complete and accurate information in support of a legitimate thesis. Do not plagiarize. Coupled with diligence, effort can make a difference.

This format of a research paper is often required in English, composition, literature, humanities, and social science courses (both undergraduate and graduate).

A Few Words About Sample Papers

This book features sample papers that provide specific instructions and examples of the essential elements required for this type of writing. For the purpose of clarity and accuracy, sample papers are double-spaced with a Times New Roman 12-point font, which is required in MLA (Modern Language Association) format.[1]

The emphasis added technique is utilized throughout this book because it is a technique you may employ in your own writing. *Here* (emphasis added) is an example. Quotation marks should not be used for the purpose of adding emphasis.

The sample papers' nature demands that the papers are short in length, often comprised of two to five paragraphs. Even though you see a three-paragraph sample paper in this book, this does not mean that a three-paragraph essay is necessarily acceptable. It all depends on the assignment requirements and the directions of your instructor.

When faced with the challenge of quoting, providing parenthetical documentation, and listing sources in the Works Cited section, the key to accuracy is to understand the rules for an example that is nearly identical to what you seek. You will find excellent practices for using quotes and parenthetical documentation in these sample papers; at times, a specific example, such as citing by title in parenthetical documentation, will appear in a sample before the chapter, which it addresses, begins.

The contents of this book are presented in a specific order for good reason; however, you will find yourself skipping around back and forth in order to find the right example for the component of critical writing that you are attempting to master.

---

1 *MLA Handbook for Writers of Research Papers* (New York: The Modern Language Association of America, 2009), 116.

Fig. P-1 Operating a Computer Keyboard MOD 45158106

LEARNING OUTCOMES

Learning outcomes are what students can expect to achieve by the time the semester ends. Outcomes are also specific tasks that will be mastered during the course of the semester. They are standard and essential components of college-level courses. Achievement of the following outcomes will be determining factors in your success.

- Analyze assignment requirements
- Utilize sources for the purpose of thesis formulation
- Formulate an argumentative and innovative thesis that can be supported
- Integrate thesis support from a variety of sources
- Determine where the strongest thesis support exists
- Construct thesis support through specific examples from multiple sources
- Demonstrate a consistent academic style of writing
- Demonstrate a mastery of MLA documentation
- Construct a complete and accurate Works Cited list
- Critique both primary and secondary sources based on their quality and relevance
- Challenge assumptions based on your topic
- Construct an organized and logically sound paper
- Organize specific ideas logically and coherently
- Use specific details for the purpose of thesis support
- Revise through self, peer, and instructor evaluation
- Use constructive and concrete terminology in review of your peers' work
- Cite sources in parenthetical documentation accurately
- Eliminate or minimize errors in grammar, punctuation, and spelling
- Employ revision and reconsideration in the process of writing
- Differentiate academic from nonacademic sources
- Demonstrate a clear and consistent purpose in your writing

BASIC GUIDELINES

- Papers written in MLA format are double-spaced throughout.
- Papers should not begin with a separate title page.
- The heading (student's name, instructor's name, class name, and date) is on the first
  page only, and all pages have the student's last name and page number (header) aligned to the right.
- Writing in the present tense and in the third person is required.
- Quotes that take up five lines or more must be in block format; block quotes are set in the middle of a paragraph, indented from the text above and below them.
- A complete sentence followed by a colon is required before a bock quote.
- A new paragraph cannot be started following a block quote.
- When multiple block quotes are used, papers must go beyond the minimum number of pages required.
- Footnotes and endnotes should not be included.
- Parenthetical documentation for specific events is required at the end of the sentence.
- Parenthetical documentation for quotes may appear immediately after the quote or at the end of the sentence.
- Sources in your Works Cited page are listed alphabetically.
- Authorless works should be introduced and cited in the parenthetical documentation
  by title.
- Every source must be quoted at least once.
- The primary source must be introduced before the thesis in the introductory paragraph by both author and title, and it will be quoted/cited multiple times.
- Authors are introduced by their first and last names; they are referred to by their last names thereafter.
- Quotes and specific events require parenthetical documentation in order to avoid plagiarism.

- MLA format requires accuracy in quotes and complete information for all sources.
- The use of contractions is unacceptable for research paper writing; *can't, didn't, won't, she's* (as in *she is*), and *he's,* (emphasis added) among other contractions, should not be present in your writing.
- Use of the ampersand (&) is not permitted.
- Write out numbers that are comprised of one or two words (three, seventy-seven, twelve hundred, nine million) in your paper. Numerals should be used for numbers that are comprised of three or more words: 6 ¾, 707, and 3,755, for example.

Sample Paper One

Page 1

Student Name

Instructor Name

Course Name and Number

Due Date

Title

This page is an example of page 1 of a paper written in MLA format. Your last name, followed by one space and the page number, is required for all pages, including the first page. The right-hand side of the margin is not justified; it is not aligned to the right side of the page like the left margin is. MLA papers are double-spaced throughout.[1] In Microsoft Word, open the *Paragraph* menu. Under the *Indents and Spacing* tab, set line spacing at double and make sure 0-pt. spacing is selected for both *Before* and *After* (emphasis added).

---

1 *MLA Handbook for Writers of Research Papers* (New York: The Modern Language Association of America, 2009), 116–17.

The initial heading, listing your first and last name, instructor's name, class name, and date, is present on page 1 only. Do not repeat the heading. Every page, including the first, will list your last name and page number in the header. Do not type page numbers at the top of the page. Instead, open the header, type your last name and align it to the right, then use the *Page Number* (emphasis added) function, so that the program can paginate your essay for you. Titles of your essays are centered and capitalized; they should not be **bolded**, *italicized*, <u>underlined</u>, or set in "quotation marks." For the font, always use Times New Roman, size 12.

Abbreviations for Months and Publisher Names

In a Works Cited page, January, February, March, April, August, September, October, November, and December may be abbreviated as follows: Jan., Feb., Mar., Apr., Aug., Sept., Oct., Nov., and Dec.[1]

May, June, and July cannot be abbreviated. Consider the fact that these month names have the same number of letters as the abbreviations for the other months do. Months should not be abbreviated in the text of your paper, including in the MLA heading located on the first page.

For Works Cited listings, publisher abbreviations are both specific and required. The objective is to list the minimal amount of information necessary. Abbreviations should also be applied to movie studios, record companies, and so on. At times, the correct publisher abbreviation is listed on the spine of a book itself. The following publishers are accurately abbreviated in the right-hand column:

Publisher	Publisher Abbreviation
University of Chicago Press	U of Chicago P
Chicago University Press	Chicago UP

---

1 *MLA Handbook for Writers of Research Papers* (New York: The Modern Language Association of America, 2016), 95.

<h1 style="text-align:center">Shortened Titles</h1>

While shortened versions of titles may not technically be abbreviations, here is a good a place as any to address them. If a title is listed often in the text of your paper, you may use a shortened version after the full title has been introduced completely. Edgar Allan Poe's "The Fall of the House of Usher" appears first, and your audience will see that "House of Usher" is the same story. "The Masque of the Red Death" is introduced; afterward "Red Death" will suffice. The key here is to remain consistent. If you have decided to use shortened titles, stick to them throughout your paper. For shorter papers, you should not utilize this method. Minimizing the repetition of titles within your paper can be achieved by making distinctions in the parenthetical documentation (see "Parenthetical Documentation: Multiple Works Written by the Same Author").

Abbreviations for Books of the Bible and Works Written by William Shakespeare

There are established title abbreviations for the Bible and Shakespeare's works because they are often used as sources. Minimizing the repetition of titles within your paper can be achieved by making distinctions in the parenthetical documentation (see "Citing by Title").

Various abbreviated books of the Bible, followed by the complete book title in parentheses (note that these titles are not italicized): Dan. (Daniel), Deut. (Deuteronomy), Exod. (Exodus), Gen. (Genesis), Isa. (Isaiah), Prov. (Proverbs), Ps. (Psalms), and Rev. (Revelation).[2]

Various abbreviated Shakespeare titles, followed by the complete title in parentheses: *Ado* (*Much Ado about Nothing*), *Ant.* (*Antony and Cleopatra*), *AYL* (*As You Like It*), *Err.* (*The Comedy of Errors*), *Ham.* (*Hamlet*), *H5* (*Henry V*), *JC* (*Julius Caesar*), *Lr.* (*King Lear*), *Mac.* (*Macbeth*), *MND* (*A Midsummer*

---

2 *MLA Handbook* (2016), 97–99.

Night's Dream), *MV* (*The Merchant of Venice*), *Oth.* (*Othello*), *R2* (*Richard II*), *R3* (*Richard III*), *Rom.* (*Romeo and Juliet*), and *Tmp.* (*The Tempest*).[3]

If the title abbreviation you seek is not listed here, an online search for the MLA abbreviation is recommended.

Apostrophes

The plural form of abbreviated nouns or numbers does not include an apostrophe: DVDs, TVs, 1960s, and 70s. Apostrophes will not be an issue for contractions because of the fact that they are not permitted. If a contraction (see page 3) is present in a quote, keep it for the sake of accuracy.

An apostrophe followed by an *s* (emphasis added) makes singular proper nouns (including nouns that end with an *s*) possessive: Ella's, Thomas's, and Daniels's.[4]

---

3   *MLA Handbook* (2016), 100–01.
4   *MLA Handbook for Writers of Research Papers* (New York: The Modern Language Association of America, 2009), 74–75.

Each required source must be introduced, quoted, and cited in parenthetical documentation and listed completely and accurately in the Works Cited section. The primary source should be introduced before the thesis in the introductory paragraph.

Secondary sources are typically critical of the primary source. Your paper may be a secondary source of its own, effectively focusing on a singular thesis with regard to the primary source. Your assignment could possibly require multiple primary sources.

Once a source has been properly introduced, it can and must be quoted primarily for the purpose of thesis support. Authors are always introduced, and primary sources are introduced by both author and title. Movies and television shows are considered to be authorless sources and are introduced by title.

Authors and other contributors whose work you will be quoting and citing must be introduced by their full names first. Beyond that introduction, these individuals are referred to only by their last names in your sentences and in the parenthetical documentation.

Titles

Authors are always listed first in a Works Cited section. Some sources are, or are considered to be, authorless. "Anonymous" should never be listed as an author. Where titles are concerned, smaller titles must be listed before the titles of larger sources in which they are contained. In a Works Cited list, we can determine what the components are by how they are punctuated, how they are formatted, and where they are located. Listings for movies and television shows begin with the title, and the writer is not listed; however, if the writer's work is the focus of your paper, he or she can be listed first in a Works Cited entry.

The first and last words of titles must be capitalized. In addition, the following must be capitalized: nouns, pronouns, verbs, adjectives, adverbs, and subordinating conjunctions. Do not capitalize articles, prepositions, coordinating conjunctions, or infinitives (e.g., "to") in the middle of a title. Religious texts and political documents are capitalized but not listed in italics or quotation marks. Refer specifically to the "Works Cited" sample paper for examples of correct capitalization. In fact, there are capitalization examples presented throughout this textbook.

Titles Presented in Italics or Quotation Marks

Source Title	→	Contained in	→	Larger Source Title
"Story, Poem, Essay, or Chapter Title"				*Book Title*
"Magazine or Newspaper Article" *or Newspaper Title*				*Magazine*
"Internet Article Title" *Online Database Title*				*Website or*
"Television Episode" *Series*				*Television*
"Song Title" *Title*				*Album*

An Epic Poem in Book Form
Movie Title
Play Title[1]

---

1 *MLA Handbook for Writers of Research Papers* (New York: The Modern Language Association of America, 2016), 68–69.

Fig. 1-1 Edward Hopper's *Nighthawks*

Sample Paper Two

Works Cited

Student Name

Instructor Name

English 102

19 March 2018

Title

A research paper assignment will include a number of required sources, which are listed alphabetically. It is wise to begin assembling the Works Cited list first in the process of completing the assignment. Oftentimes, students make additions to and revise their Works Cited page at the last minute, right before it is due, causing errors that result in point deduction. You may not know what your thesis is; however, you should begin your work in a substantial way by listing required sources. If you have a choice between a few required sources, even if one or more listing needs to be removed/switched for another source, at least you will have had more practice in listing these sources completely and accurately according to MLA format. Again, if you know what the required sources are before you begin writing, you should start with the Works Cited section.

There are strict rules for what goes where, and how things must appear, along with spacing, punctuation, and capitalization (or the lack thereof). Note that two names listed before a title require a comma before the word *and* (emphasis added); however, for two names listed after the title, the comma is not present. Contributors—who are not the authors—whose contributions are the focus of your paper can be listed first in a Works Cited section. *Anonymous* (emphasis added) will never be listed for an authorless source. Begin the listing with the title when there is no author. The format allows for a contributor (a director or performer in a film, or an artist of a comic book/graphic novel, for example) who is the focus of your paper (but not the author) to be listed first. While page ranges are required, time ranges for audio and video sources should not be listed in a Works Cited section. The correct abbreviations for

months and words, such as *edition* and *volume* (emphasis added),

may be listed in a Works Cited section.

Punctuation must be added to the components for each Works

Cited entry: periods at the end of the author name(s), source title,

original publication year, and final component listed. Periods will

typically appear for the first, second, and last part of a source listed.

Commas should be present at the end of all other information listed,

particularly following the larger source (book, website, television

series, album, etc.) if it exists.[1] Movie titles stand alone, and the

period is required. Numerous sources are listed in the Works Cited

section here with color-coded information that explains what the

examples are demonstrating. Although some numerals are unac-

ceptable in your paragraphs (see page 3), they are permitted, for the

purpose of accuracy, in a Works Cited list.

---

1 *MLA Handbook for Writers of Research Papers* (New York: The Modern
Language Association of America, 2016), 20.

Works Cited

Abrams, J. J., director. *Star Wars: The Force Awakens*. Performances by

Daisy Ridley, John Boyega, Adam Driver, Carrie Fisher, and Harrison

Ford, Disney, 2016.

The director's work is the focus of this paper for this source.

American Cancer Society. "Diet and Physical Activity: What's the

Cancer Connection?" *Cancer.org*, 2 February 2016, www.cancer.

org/cancer/cancercauses/dietandphysicalactivity/diet-and-physical-

activity.

The American Cancer Society is a corporate author, so no

individual author's name was listed for this article.

Date of latest update (publication).

Bastien, Angelica Jade. Review of *Doctor Strange*, directed by Scott

Derrickson, *Rogerebert.com*, 4 November 2016, www.rogerebert.com/

reviews/doctor-strange-2016.

An online movie review.

Bolland, Brian, artist and colorist. *Batman: The Killing Joke*. 1988.

Written by Alan Moore, lettered by Richard Starkings, deluxe ed., DC

Comics, 2008, pp. 1–46.

Bolland is the comic book contributor whose work is the focus
of the paper for this source.

Brooks, Rodney. "Duck! Here Comes the Boomerang." *USA Today*, 22
October 2013, pp. 1B+.

Due to the fact that the second page of the article appears on
a nonconsecutive page to the first page (1B), it is represented
by the plus sign. The plus sign replaces any number or range of
additional pages which are not consecutive to the first page.

"The Dark at the End of the Tunnel." *Daredevil*, performances by Charlie
Cox, Deborah Ann Woll, and Jon Bernthal, season 2, episode 12,
Marvel Television, 18 March 2016, *Netflix.*

There is no URL available because the episode was viewed on
the Netflix app, where there is no address bar present.

Del Toro, Guillermo. *"Hellboy II: The Golden Army." Cabinet of
Curiosities: My Notebooks, Collections, and Other Obsessions*, Harper
Design, 2013, pp. 133–73.

An example of a title within title (a chapter title that is also a movie title).

Dini, Paul, writer. "Choosing Sides." *Batman: Arkham City*, illustrated and cover art by Carlos D'Anda, colored by Gabe Eltaeb, lettered by Travis Lanham, no. 3, DC Comics, August 2011, pp. 1–20.

An issue number (the "no." abbreviation for "number" should always be used) of a comic book series.

Twenty pages of the story counted (advertisement pages skipped).

Dyer, Ben, editor. "The Wandering Unwanted." *Supervillains and Philosophy: Sometimes, Evil Is Its Own Reward*, Open Court, 2009, pp. 3–11.

Editor as author.

"Escape from Earth-2." *The Flash*, performances by Grant Gustin, Danielle Panabaker, Carlos Valdes, and Tom Cavanagh, season 2, episode 14, The CW Television Network, 16 February 2016.

This episode of *The Flash* was viewed on a television; a DVR

recording makes quotes and time codes for parenthetical

documentation simple.

Goodell, Jeff. "Gore's Grim Prophecy." *Rolling Stone,* no. 1177, 28

February 2013, pp. 39–42.

A magazine with both an issue number and date of

publication.

Homer. "Book 11: The Kingdom of the Dead." *The Odyssey,* translated by

Robert Fagles, Penguin Books, 1996, pp. 249–70.

The Odyssey is an epic poem with titled books/sections.

Hubler, Edward. "The Economy of the Closed Heart." *Shakespeare:*

Modern Essays in Criticism, edited by Leonard F. Dean, Oxford UP,

pp. 467–76.

Abbreviation for *University Press* (emphasis added).

Jaworski, Michelle. "Bear Relaxes in Vancouver Couple's Pool and Hot

Tub." *Msn.com,* 19 August 2015, www.msn.com/en-us/news/offbeat/

bear-relaxes-in-vancouver-couples-pool-and-hot-tub/ar-BBlS550.

Capitalization errors fixed.

May, Brian, et al., performers. "Stone Cold Crazy." *Sheer Heart Attack,*

Elektra Records, 1974.

For more than three authors who are also performers, the first

name (Brian May) is listed, and the remaining three names

(Freddie Mercury, Roger Taylor, and John Deacon) are replaced

by *et al.* (emphasis added).

Mercer, Johnny. "Something's Gotta Give." *Come Dance with Me!*

Performance by Frank Sinatra, Capitol Records, 1959.

The exclamation mark replaces the comma, which would

normally follow the larger title; therefore, the *p* in *performance*

(emphasis added) is capitalized for this exception to the

rules.

Mercury, Freddie, performer. "Don't Stop Me Now." *Jazz*, performances

by Brian May, Roger Taylor, and John Deacon, Elektra Records,

1978.

---, performer. "Somebody to Love." *A Day at the Races*, performances by

Brian May, Roger Taylor, and John Deacon, Elektra Records, 1976.

The three hyphens replace the name Freddie Mercury to show

that his name is repeated from the previous reference.

Moore, Alan, writer. *Batman: The Killing Joke*. 1988. Art and colors by

Brian Bolland, lettered by Richard Starkings, deluxe edition, DC

Comics, 2008, pp. 1–46.

Although the word *writer* (emphasis added) may be redundant

for Alan Moore, it is important to list contributors and their

roles as articulated in the original comic book.

Poe, Edgar Allan. "The Black Cat." 1843. *Edgar Allan Poe: The Complete

Stories*, Everyman's Library, 1992, pp. 648–56.

This Poe story is listed first because we do not alphabetize by the articles *a*, *an*, or *the* (emphasis added).

The original year of publication.

---. "The Masque of the Red Death." 1842. *Edgar Allan Poe: The Complete Stories*, Everyman's Library, 1992, pp. 604–09.

Two or more sources written by the same author/the three hyphens replace the name Edgar Allan Poe.

The number 6 is omitted for page 609.

---. "The Murders in the Rue Morgue." 1841. *Edgar Allan Poe: The Complete Stories*, Everyman's Library, 1992, pp. 473–505.

"Rupture." *The Flash*, performances by Grant Gustin, Danielle Panabaker, Carlos Valdes, and Tom Cavanagh, season 2, episode 20, The CW Television Network, 16 February 2016. *CWTV*, www.cwtv.com/shows/the-flash/rupture/?play=e18d5546-e2cb-4256-a3ea-b1a980747dbd.

Salisbury, Mark. Crimson Peak: *The Art of Darkness*. Insight Editions, 2015, pp. 1–160.

A movie title that is not italicized because it is part of the book title (a title within a title).

Seelye, John, introduction. *Edgar Allan Poe: The Complete Stories*. By Edgar Allan Poe, Everyman's Library, 1992, pp. vii–xxi.

@SenSanders. "It's not right that despite an increase in worker productivity for decades, the average worker is working longer hours for lower wages." *Twitter*, 1 June 2016, 1:23 p.m.

Bernie Sanders's tweet doubles as the title (with no capitalization corrections for it) and with the Twitter app, a URL is unavailable.

Waggoner, John. "What's an Investor to Do?" *USA Today*, 8 Oct. 2013, p. 1B.

Wright, Bradford. "Batman." *St. James Encyclopedia of Popular Culture*, edited by Thomas Riggs, 2nd ed., vol. 1, St. James P, 2013, pp. 229–31.

Gale Virtual Reference Library, go.galegroup.com/ps/i.do?id=GAL

E%7CCX2735800205&v=2.1&u=chic13716&it=r&p=GVRL&sw

=w&asid=e88b56b87e47e778e5121784ce03334c.

Some URLs (note the lack of an apostrophe for URLs) are

deficient in forward slashes, so the aesthetics take precedence

over the rule of hitting return only after a slash.

Comic Books

Comic books are also referred to as *graphic novels* or *graphic narratives* (emphasis added). They feature the work of multiple contributors. Their roles are specifically worded, and they should be listed accurately in a Works Cited section, as opposed to being grouped together as *et al* (emphasis added). Contributors have also been known to have multiple roles. Here the placement of other contributors[1] is combined with the original articulation of their roles.[2] Editors may be omitted (unless you are instructed to include them). Comic book stories are originally featured in a single issue of the series; they are also smaller parts of a larger book, known as a trade paperback (or trade hardcover, depending on book format).

Stern, Roger, writer and co-plotter. "By the Dawn's Early Light!" 1980. *Marvel Universe by John Byrne*, penciled and co-plotted by John Byrne, inked by Josef Rubinstein, lettered by Jim Novak, colored by George Roussos, Marvel Comics, 2016, pp. 499–516.

John Byrne's contributions are the focus of this paper, prompting his name to be listed first. Roger Stern is listed after the book title.

Byrne, John, penciler and co-plotter. "By the Dawn's Early Light!" 1980. *Marvel Universe by John Byrne*, written and co-plotted by Roger Stern, inked by Josef Rubinstein, lettered by Jim Novak, colored by George Roussos, Marvel Comics, 2016, pp. 499–516.

---

1 *MLA Handbook* (2016), 37.
2 *MLA Handbook for Writers of Research Papers* (New York: The Modern Language Association of America, 2009), 166.

---, story and art. "Choices." *Fantastic Four*, colored by Glynis Wein, lettered by Jim

Novak, no. 259, Marvel Comics, October 1983, pp. 1–22.

Marvel Universe by John Byrne is a book, so "By the Dawn's Early Light!" is listed as a comic book story in a book. "Choices" is an individual issue of *Fantastic Four*. With no page numbers present, twenty-two pages are counted.

While the existence of a formula for generating a legitimate thesis is hard to come by, there are ways of making thesis generation simpler.

Secondary sources often contain claims/opinions that can be argued against, thus resulting in a thesis. Simply put, if you prove that a particular statement/claim that a person is making is incorrect, you may have a thesis. Agreeing with someone, presenting compare-and-contrast information (actually, the contrast may be represented by the secondary source you are arguing against), or summarizing will not result in a legitimate thesis or an argumentative paper.

Imagine that you are a lawyer who is either defending or prosecuting; your success will depend on the strength of your argument and your ability to utilize key evidence to support your assertion. Being neutral on the issue is not an option. You cannot argue both for and against something.

The complication lies in finding a claim to argue against, with sufficient support from the other required sources for the length of the paper. For example, if your paper is going to be five pages in length, not including the Works Cited section, you must ask yourself if there is enough support for your thesis to complete the page requirement. This question applies to every research paper/critical analysis/argumentative paper with required sources that you will be instructed to write.

Presenting a bit of contrast from the side you are arguing against is a good idea, especially in a paper of considerable length. Students often find themselves needing to tack on more to their papers in order to meet the page requirement.

The thesis is often the last or second-to-last sentence of the introductory paragraph. For a longer paper, it acceptable for the thesis to be in the second or third paragraph; however, you should follow instructions if thesis placement is a specific requirement. Either way, it should be obvious what your thesis is, and it must be a legitimate one.

Sample Paper Three

One Primary Source / Cross-Referencing Two
Secondary Sources in the Works Cited

Last Name 1

Student Name

Instructor Name

Literature 157

23 December 2017

Pointless

Alan Moore's *Batman: The Killing Joke* provides an opportunity for a concrete and accessible example of a thesis as well as the components that surround it in a critical paper. Introduction of the primary source and its author has been established in the first sentence. We must accept certain truths in this analysis: the Joker fails to prove his point that tragedy drives people mad, and the fact that murder and cruelty are inexcusable, making sympathy for this particular perpetrator impossible. Using the specific question method for thesis generation is simple. The question is not whether the Joker fails to "prove a [his] point" (Moore 14); it is *why* (emphasis added) he fails. The Joker's failure is the result of refusing to accept the existence of his own free will, which is demonstrated by both Batman and Commissioner Gordon. The Clown Prince of Crime's point is completely invalid.

With no page numbers present, forty-six pages have been counted to provide informative parenthetical documentation. Interestingly enough, this sample paper may contain more words than the actual story does. When quoting a comic book, all caps should be avoided, and setting particular words present in the original source boldface is encouraged. Here, an ellipsis, with a space before and after, signals that part of this quote has been omitted, and it is introduced by a complete sentence, so the colon is required here: "It's all a **joke!** … It's all a **monstrous**, demented **gag!**" (Moore 39). Do not use the terms *crazy* or *insane* (emphasis added) in your writing. However, feel free to quote these terms: The Joker asserts that going "stark slavering buggo!" (*sic*) and that "any **other** response would be **crazy!**" are necessary to survive in a cruel, meaningless world (Moore 33). Do not summarize or retell the story of *Batman: The Killing Joke.* Events, best

identified with phenomenal quotes, are presented as thesis support.

Facts and events that have nothing to do with the thesis do not belong

in a critical paper.

The Joker's twisted worldview and vile deeds are symptomatic

of an individual who refuses to accept responsibility for the choices

he has made: "If I'm going to have a past, I prefer it to be multiple-

choice!" (Moore 39). Batman and Commissioner Gordon believe

that the importance of law and order assumes precedence over the

chaos inflicted on them:

> BATMAN. Listen, the **police** are following right **behind**
>
> me ... I'll stay here with you until they **arrive**.
>
> GORDON. **No!** I'm **okay!** **You** have to go after **him**! I want
>
> him **brought in** ... and I want him brought in by the **book**!
>
> BATMAN. I'll do my best.

GORDON. By the **book**, you **hear**? We have to **show** him!

We have to show him that our way **works**! (Moore 37)[1]

The technique of quoting dialogue from a play or screenplay has been utilized for *Batman: The Killing Joke*. Note the format of quoting dialogue and how it is introduced; the placement is the center of a well-developed paragraph.

A secondary source will be introduced by author here in order to present an example of a block quote. The block quote format is required when the quote takes up five or more lines. The quote must be introduced by a complete sentence, which ends in a colon. Galen Foresman documents that the Joker is aware of this realization:

> … being the best of the worst means failing big time. The Joker has probably the best understanding of this fine point. He goes to great lengths to make sure that he enjoys and takes pride in his wacky schemes. In fact, he seems to

---

1 *MLA Handbook for Writers of Research Papers* (New York: The Modern Language Association of America, 2016), 80.

have ditched most lofty goals altogether and instead focuses almost entirely on toying with his rival, bat-brains. (29)

This paragraph must be completed with two or three sentences before a new paragraph can begin. Here, another secondary source is introduced by author and quoted with the required parenthetical documentation. Daniel Moseley makes the distinction that "any discussion of the Joker involves determining which representations of the Joker are relevant" (127).

The Works Cited section features cross-referencing, which can be employed when there are multiple sources (two secondary sources, Foresman and Moseley, for this sample paper) present in the same collection and listed in the Works Cited section. The presence of an editor is preferred; the editor (or editors—the presence of multiple editors does occur) of the anthology, Ben Dyer, provides the reference point for the other listings in the form of the complete Works

Cited listing. Secondary sources should not be tacked on at the end of a critical paper. Here the final paragraphs are meant for the purpose of demonstrating block quoting and cross-referencing.

Works Cited

Dyer, Ben, editor. *Supervillains and Philosophy: Sometimes, Evil Is Its Own Reward.* Open Court, 2009.

Foresman, Galen. "Making the A-List." Dyer, *Supervillains and Philosophy*, pp. 23–30.

Moore, Alan, writer. *Batman: The Killing Joke.* 1988. Art and colors by Brian Bolland, lettered by Richard Starkings, deluxe edition, DC Comics, 2008, pp. 1–46.

Moseley, Daniel. "The Joker's Comedy of Existence." Dyer, *Supervillains and Philosophy*, pp. 127–36.

Sample Paper Four

Multiple Primary Sources / One Secondary Source

Last Name 1

Student

Instructor

English 1302

15 December 2017

Title

This paper will focus on three short stories written by Edgar Allan Poe for the purpose of thesis support. John Seelye's assertion of "contrived cosmopolitanism" and Poe's "obsession with sin, madness, and death" (xx) from his introduction (a secondary source) will be argued against in order to generate a legitimate thesis. Poe should be introduced first; John Seelye is then introduced and quoted, with the page number present in the parenthetical documentation. The thesis (one complete sentence with no quotes) follows, and Poe stories with the strongest examples of thesis support are introduced by title: "The Black Cat" and "The Murders in the Rue Morgue," for example.

"The Masque of the Red Death" must be introduced further along in a later paragraph. This paper may also require demonstration of listing multiple works written by the same author in parenthetical documentation (see pages 81-83). It is important to refrain from listing these short stories in your sentences over and over again, especially in a paper of considerable length. Here, the narrative examination—in "The Murders in the Rue Morgue" of "analytical power"—counteracts the generalization of an "obsession with sin, madness and death" (Poe 475; Seelye ix).[1] Dupin demonstrates his significant power of observation, a skill required for detective work:

> NARRATOR. I do not hesitate to say that I am amazed, and can scarcely credit my senses. How was it possible you should know I was thinking of—?
>
> DUPIN. —of Chantilly ... why do you pause? You were remarking to yourself that his diminutive figure unfitted him for tragedy.

---

1 *MLA Handbook for Writers of Research Papers* (New York: The Modern Language Association of America, 2016), 58.

NARRATOR. Tell me, for Heaven's sake ... the method—

if method there is—by which you have been enabled to

fathom my soul in this matter.

DUPIN. It was the fruiterer [sic] ... who brought you to the

conclusion that the mender of soles was not of sufficient

height for Xerxes ... ("Murders" 478)

With multiple primary sources that provide thesis support, quotes

from two stories per paragraph is highly recommended. How the

thesis is supported determines the integration of these quotes.

Imagine that this supporting paragraph features a quote from "The

Black Cat" and "The Murders in the Rue Morgue."

You may find yourself writing three paragraphs that simply

summarize Poe's three stories, which is unwise. The goal is to avoid

summarization. Do not retell the stories or set up the context of

scenes. Presenting thesis support from two different stories per

paragraph will be of great assistance in avoiding summarization.

The Works Cited list features cross-referencing, which can be employed when there are two or more sources (three short stories, for this sample paper) present in the same collection and listed in the Works Cited section. The presence of an editor is preferred; the editor (or editors—the presence of multiple editors does occur) of the anthology provides the reference point for the other listings in the form of the complete Works Cited listing.

Here, Seeyle's introduction serves as a secondary source and the complete Works Cited listing and, as the author of the introduction, may be likened to an editor. Note that the name Seeyle has been added, and a shortened title has replaced the book title, while the publisher Everyman's Library and the original year, 1992, have been omitted for the Poe listings.

Works Cited

Poe, Edgar Allan. "The Black Cat." 1843. Seelye, *Complete Stories*, pp.

648–56.

---. "The Masque of the Red Death." 1842. Seeyle, *Complete Stories*, pp.

604–09.

---. "The Murders in the Rue Morgue." 1841. Seeyle, *Complete Stories*, pp.

473–505.

Seelye, John, introduction. *Edgar Allan Poe: The Complete Stories.* By

Edgar Allan Poe, Everyman's Library, 1992, pp. vii–xxi.

Critical Analysis and Writing Style

Research papers/critical analysis assignments must be written in the present tense (but do not change the tense of quotes) and in the third person; avoiding the first person means no appearances of *I, me,* or *my* (emphasis added) in your writing.

Do not make announcements—for example, *This paper will explore…* or *This thesis is…* (emphasis added).

The introduction is often the prime location for generalizations, which may be untrue, so do not use terms such as *none, never, all, always,* and *every* (emphasis added).

Do not prove a negative. Argue and demonstrate what something is as opposed to what it is not.

Avoid using conversational terms such as *a lot* or *really* (emphasis added).

Consistency and accuracy are immensely important throughout your paper, especially in the Works Cited list.

Parenthetical documentation for quotes can immediately follow the quote or appear at the end of the sentence where the quote is introduced.

Remove the term *rough draft* (emphasis added) from your mind. Put forth your best effort to assemble as perfect a paper (format-wise) as possible.

Peer Reviews

Peer reviews are an important part of revision. You may work with your classmates during peer reviews conducted in class or outside of class on your own time. While it is vital that you master the ability to reproduce how a critical (MLA-format) paper should appear, never copy your classmates' work. Copying is considered to be plagiarism. Do not allow anyone to leave class with a copy of your paper, and do not email your work to your classmates.

Mastering this type of writing does require the ability to produce your own work completely and accurately based on the guidelines and rules of MLA format. Classes are communities, and working together and discussing assignments are what learning communities do.

AVOIDING PLAGIARISM / COMMON KNOWLEDGE VS. CITATION

Copying and pasting someone else's writing/ideas into your paper is never acceptable. There is only one exception: the copying and pasting of a URL when it is required in a Works Cited listing for an Internet source (see pages 22, 26, 28, and 30).

Three things are essential to avoiding plagiarism with the use of required sources: (1) We must know who the author is, or what the title is for an authorless source. (2) Quotes always require citation. They must be written word for word within quotation marks. (3) Parenthetical documentation is required as well.

Even with the same sources and a similar thesis, it is highly unlikely that two students will have the exact same thesis (word for word) and examples for thesis support. Writing an argumentative paper with diligence and honest intent is the best way to avoid plagiarism. Simply do not plagiarize, and do not take any shortcuts. Do not copy your classmates' work, either. Copying something as simple as a paper title can be considered plagiarism.

The determination of whether something is common knowledge or in need of citation is based on whichever topic your critical paper is addressing. When information needs citation, the three components needed to avoid plagiarism are required. The use of quotes and the listing of specific events require citation.

Statistics and controversial statements that cannot be found in most sources require citation.

Sample Paper Five

Common Knowledge vs. Citation Example

Last Name 1

Student

Instructor

English 1312

5 April 2016

Title

In order to differentiate common knowledge from citation, we can use *Star Wars: The Force Awakens* as an example. The fact that events in this movie take place three decades after *Return of the Jedi* is considered to be common knowledge. The plot of *The Force Awakens* centers on the search for Luke Skywalker, which is common knowledge. The italicized title of the legendary *Millennium Falcon* spacecraft is common knowledge. Specific quotes and events from the film must be cited. Introducing characters and planets does not require quotation marks or parenthetical documentation, unless this introduction is part of an actual quote. Recall that the topic determines what common knowledge is.

Listing the film's worldwide revenue total as of late January 2016, $1.9 billion, in this manner—minus quotation marks, and any reference to Scott Mendelson—can be considered plagiarism, even if he is properly introduced, quoted, and cited elsewhere in your paper. Here we introduce and quote the writer, and plagiarism is avoided: Scott Mendelson notes that the box office take of *The Force Awakens* in January 2016 was "around $1.9 billion." Quotation marks and proper documentation are required for two reasons: the information is written word for word from the original source, and the information is statistical. Mendelson has been introduced and quoted (see above); here his last name is listed in the parenthetical documentation, and plagiarism is avoided once again: This immensely successful "film never had to break every single box office record to be a top-tier victory" (Mendelson) for the studio.

Specific quotes and events require citation. Citing a specific event in the form of an important quote is recommended. Han Solo informs Finn of what is obvious to any *Star Wars* aficionado, declaring, "That's not *how* the Force works!" (emphasis added) based on his transformation from nonbeliever to believer in the Force's existence (*Star* 01:37:07–09).[1]

---

1 *MLA Handbook for Writers of Research Papers* (New York: The Modern Language Association of America, 2016), 56–57.

Works Cited

Mendelson, Scott. "Box Office: *Star Wars: The Force Awakens* Isn't

Topping *Avatar* Worldwide, and That's Okay." *Forbes.com*, 22 January

2016, www.forbes.com/sites/scottmendelson/2016/01/22/box-office-

star-wars-the-force-awakens-isnt-topping-avatar-worldwide-and-

thats-okay/#2a7557785ca6.

Star Wars: The Force Awakens, directed by J. J. Abrams, performances by

Daisy Ridley, John Boyega, Adam Driver, and Harrison Ford, Disney,

2016.

QUOTES

Says, tells, states, said, saying, told, telling, stated, and *stating* (emphasis added) should not be used for the purpose of introducing quotes. Utilize superior and more descriptive present-tense words that provide context to introduce quotes: *declares, exclaims, insinuates, reveals, observes, questions, screams, informs, cries, divulges, discloses, enlightens, advises, notifies, notes,* and *whispers* (emphasis added) for example.

A search for synonyms in Microsoft Word or an old-fashioned thesaurus can assist you in finding the superior word you seek. Better wording for introducing quotes demonstrates better word choices, which may result in a higher grade.

Always be specific. Less is definitely more when it comes to quotes. The best and most essential parts of the best quotes should be put into context in one sentence. A shorter quote will help ensure that the importance of the quote is demonstrated in that one sentence. You must demonstrate why this quote is important and necessary for thesis support.

An ellipsis, composed of three periods and the appropriate spaces, should be used if a phrase is omitted from a quote (see page 38). A word or phrase needed for clarification may be presented in square brackets within a quote (see page 37). Adding emphasis with italics (and a parenthetical note about the added emphasis at the end of the sentence) to a word or phrase is more effective and correct than utilizing single or double quotation marks alone (see page 38). Listing "sic" in parentheses is a technique used to reassure the reader that a word that appears to be nonexistent or misspelled is spelled accurately according to the source (see page 38).

There should be a limit to the number of quotes per paragraph. Supporting paragraphs should include two to three quotes, without taking up too many lines in each paragraph. In other words, if your quotes amount to four lines of text in a twelve-line paragraph, you need to be more precise. The bulk of these paragraphs should be your writing, not made up of excessive quoting. With multiple primary sources that provide thesis support, quotes from two (or three) sources per paragraph is highly recommended. It will help avoid summarization and make for a more dynamic paper.

Quotes that make up five or more lines in your paper must be presented as block quotes (see pages 40, 41, and 74). These quotes are in the middle of a paragraph and introduced with a complete sentence, which must end in a colon. A new paragraph cannot be started following a block quote. Three to four complete sentences are needed to complete the paragraph. When multiple block quotes are used in a paper of significant length (ten pages or more), the final draft should go proportionally beyond the page requirement.

Sample Paper Six

A Simple Revision

Student

Instructor

Composition II

19 March 2017

A Simple Revision

Rear Window is the primary and single source for this sample paper (example). A common error, which seems to be instinctual among many students, can be found in this example: Stella provides her own "homespun philosophy" (*Rear* 00:08:55–56). This shows that her wisdom is the center of the film.

Successful revision is cause for a new paragraph and presented in the next sentence: Stella provides her own "homespun philosophy" (*Rear* 00:08:55–56), which demonstrates the fact that her wisdom serves as the film's center. Note that the parenthetical documentation may immediately follow the quote or be placed at the end of the sentence. The movie title is not present in the sentence and has already been introduced; therefore, *Rear Window* must be cited by title in the parentheses. This revision exhibits a more complex sentence, which provides superior context for a very important quote. Combining two sentences into one and exchanging *this* for *which* (emphasis added) provides a significant revision. Remember that writing is a process.

For the *Rear Window* quote, "We've become a race of Peeping Toms," the time code alone in the parenthetical documentation will suffice because the movie title is present in this sentence (00:08:45–47). Note that the listing of time codes is not required in the Work Cited entry for *Rear Window.*

Work Cited

Rear Window. 1954. Directed by Alfred Hitchcock, performances by

James Stewart, Grace Kelly, Thelma Ritter, and Wendell Corey,

Paramount Pictures, 2014.

Sample Paper Seven

Quoting Poetry and Song Lyrics

Student

Instructor

Composition II

28 January 2018

Quoting Poetry and Song Lyrics

Homer's *The Odyssey* is an epic poem in book form, which requires its title to be listed in italics. Typically, poems are works that are shorter in length than books and are included in a larger collection or anthology in book form. If posted online, the name of the website is the larger form, which will be listed in the Works Cited section. Quotes of one to three lines should be presented in this manner, with breaks (slashes) separating the lines: "So we stood there, trading heartsick stories, / deep in grief, as the tears streamed down our faces" (Homer 11.528–29).[1] In the parenthetical documentation for poetry, the line numbers are listed after the

------

1 *MLA Handbook for Writers of Research Papers* (New York: The Modern Language Association of America, 2016), 77.

book number (11) and a period. Inclusive page ranges of the poem or titled section for an epic poem are listed in the Works Cited section.

Poetry quotations that are comprised of four or more lines must be presented in an identical fashion to block quoting. Recall that the block format is required for quotes of five lines or more:

> By god, I'd rather slave on earth for another man—
>
> some dirt-poor tenant farmer who scrapes to keep alive—
>
> than rule down here over all the breathless dead.
>
> But come tell me the news about my gallant son.
>
> Did he make his way to the wars,
>
> Did the boy become a champion—yes or no? (11.556–61)

In order to complete this paragraph, Edgar Allan Poe's "Annabel Lee" will be considered an additional primary source. In this case, line numbers are not present, so counting has occurred, which can be expected for a work of reasonable length: "And this maiden she lived with no other thought / Than to love and be loved by me"

(5–6). This poem is part of a larger collection of Poe's short stories and poetry.

Similar to poetry, song lyrics are broken down into lines, complete with breaks in between. Mick Jagger and Keith Richards begin their epic "Jumping Jack Flash" with "I was born in a cross-fire hurricane / And I howled at my ma in the driving rain" (00:00:25–37), which contributes to the rebellious and tumultuous nature of the Rolling Stones. With "The End of the Beginning," Ozzy Osbourne, Tony Iommi, and Geezer Butler ask, "Is this the end of the beginning? / Or the beginning of the end?" signaling their final three years as a touring band (00:01:11–28). Periods of being forgotten and under-estimated were foretold: "I was washed up and left for dead" (Jagger and Richards 00:02:03–06). "Reanimation of your cyber sonic soul" (Butler et al. 00:04:01–07) provides a prime example of listing three or more authors in the parenthetical documentation.

Works Cited

Butler, Geezer, et al., performers. "The End of the Beginning." *13*,

performance by Brad Wilk, Republic Records, 2013.

Homer. *The Odyssey*. Translated by Robert Fagles, Penguin Books, 1996,

pp. 249–70.

Jagger, Mick, and Keith Richards, performers. "Jumping Jack Flash." 1968.

Grrr! Performances by Charlie Watts, Brian Jones, and Bill Wyman,

Interscope Records, 2012.

Poe, Edgar Allan. "Annabel Lee." 1849. *"The Raven": Tales and Poems*,

Penguin Horror, 2013, pp. 311–12.

PARENTHETICAL DOCUMENTATION

Parenthetical documentation is required for quotes as well as for specific events and ideas (all three items need citation and are not considered to be common knowledge); it is a mandatory component in avoiding plagiarism. Once required sources have been introduced, parenthetical documentation rules are utilized to provide information in an efficient manner. The repetition of titles is avoided, and the distinction between sources is provided in the parentheses.

The utilization of page numbers is essential. For print sources that do not have page numbers, it is recommended that you count the pages and establish page numbers within reason. You should not be expected to count hundreds of pages. Post-it notes marking every page with a number is a good idea. If an article or short story is in the form of a PDF file, and no page numbers are present in the original source, use the PDF page numbers embedded in the file.

Listings of time ranges for audio (songs) and video (television and film) must be present in the parenthetical documentation. Refer to the examples on pages 61, 67-68, 75, and 90. A quote with a range of time that begins in one minute and ends in the next minute should be cited in the parenthetical documentation like this: (00:03:58–04:01). Note that these time ranges should not be listed in a Works Cited entry.

Sample Paper Eight

Multiple Works Written by the Same Author

Student

Instructor

English 102

31 October 2017

Title

This section doubles as a sample paper. For the following example, Grant Morrison is the author of this particular secondary source; titles of secondary sources should not be introduced in the paper. Assume that there will be one or more primary sources introduced, quoted, and cited in parenthetical documentation. Here we can distinguish between Morrison's chapters. When multiple sources written by the same author are introduced, quoted, and cited in a paper, the format should be utilized to its fullest potential, which helps demonstrate a mastery of this level of writing. Morrison defines this event as "the official stepping stone to overseas recognition" ("Zenith" 207), which is a monumental first step.

In the previous sentence, a one-word chapter title provides a perfect and simple example of distinguishing the chapter, from which this quote is taken, in the parenthetical documentation. Here, there is no need for Morrison in the parentheses because his name is present in the sentence.

Ruben Diaz is described as "a human fusillade of passion and positivity" by the legendarily innovative comic book writer (Morrison, "What's" 291).[1] Here, a lengthy chapter title has been boiled down to one distinct word. With these articles, you must list the first distinctive word in the title for the parenthetical documentation. In 1939, Batman was introduced as "a dramatic figure with the outstretched scalloped wings of a giant bat" (Morrison, "Sun" 19) and enormously important shifts in popular culture would follow over the coming decades. Morrison draws the following parallel: "It

---

1 *MLA Handbook for Writers of Research Papers* (New York: The Modern Language Association of America, 2016), 55.

was Batman as Dracula ... preying on the even more unwholesome creatures of the night" ("Sun" 22).

Assume that Felix Tallon and Jerry Walls, authors of an additional secondary source, have been introduced earlier in this paper. Here is an example of two authors listed in parenthetical documentation: "The solid and sturdy morality of yesteryear has been replaced with a postmodern drama" (Tallon and Walls 209).

Works Cited

Morrison, Grant. "The Sun God and the Dark Knight." *Supergods: What Masked Vigilantes, Miraculous Mutants, and a Sun God from Smallville Can Teach Us about Being Human*, Spiegel and Grau, 2011, pp. 3–26.

---. "What's So Funny about Truth, Justice, and the American Way?" *Supergods: What Masked Vigilantes, Miraculous Mutants, and a Sun God from Smallville Can Teach Us about Being Human*, Spiegel and Grau, 2011, pp. 289–305.

---. "Zenith." *Supergods: What Masked Vigilantes, Miraculous Mutants, and a Sun God from Smallville Can Teach Us about Being Human*, Spiegel and Grau, 2011, pp. 207–28.

Tallon, Felix, and Jerry Walls. "Superman and *Kingdom Come*: The Surprise of Philosophical Theology." *Superheroes and Philosophy: Truth, Justice, and the Socratic Way*, edited by Tom Morris and Matt Morris, Open Court, 2008, pp. 207–20.

Two authors where the comma before *and* (emphasis

added) is required.

A book title is part of the essay title.

Sample Paper Nine

Citing by Title

Student

Instructor

English 102

28 January 2018

Title

While sources such as movies and television series episodes are written by someone, for the purpose of introduction and citation in parenthetical documentation, these sources are considered to be authorless. Like authorless sources, they must be introduced and cited by title.[1] When you cite a source by title, as with multiple works written by the same author in parenthetical documentation, there is only one right answer for what appears in the parentheses. *Pacific Rim* and "The Joker Is Wild" must be introduced before they are quoted and cited by title in the parenthetical documentation. The Clown Prince of Crime begins by announcing, "And now,

---

1 *MLA Handbook for Writers of Research Papers* (New York: The Modern Language Association of America, 2016), 55–56.

people of Gotham City, the moment you have all been waiting for" ("Joker" 00:23:32–37) in his typical narcissistic manner. Pentecost delivers, "We are cancelling the apocalypse!" (*Pacific* 01:47:11–15) with the determination and bravado his pilots have come to know and depend on.

Works Cited

"The Joker Is Wild." 1966. *Batman*, directed by Don Weis, performances by Adam West, Cesar Romero, and Burt Ward, season 1, episode 5, Warner Brothers, 2014, *Flixster*.

Pacific Rim. Directed by Guillermo Del Toro, performances by Charlie Hunnam, Rinko Kikuchi, Idris Elba, and Ron Perlman, Legendary Pictures, 2013.

Framework

Think of this framework as a blueprint for your paper. It is one that should be adapted to suit your needs and the requirements of the assignment as well as your instructor's preferences. It can be transformed into a very detailed outline. Maintain the organization here and adopt it as you write and revise:

- MLA Heading
- Creative Title
- Introduction
    - Introduce the primary source(s).
- Thesis
- Supporting Paragraphs
    - Introduce, quote, and cite writers and sources that have not been introduced yet.
    - Introduce the best brief quotes that support the thesis.
    - Save your strongest thesis support, from the best source, for last.
- Conclusion
- Works Cited
    - Sources must be listed completely and accurately according to MLA format requirements.

Checklist

From the beginning and throughout the writing process, strive to make as few errors as possible. Of course, some old habits die hard. During peer reviews and before the final draft is due, use this checklist (additional criteria specific to the requirements of the assignment and class as well as the expectations of your instructor will be provided). Go over your paper multiple times and look for two or three types of errors at a time. Mark what needs to be fixed and, if possible, make immediate revisions. The Works Cited list should be perfect, but double check it just in case revisions are needed.

- Set the paper double-spaced, with no extra space anywhere (i.e., with 0 pt. before and after paragraphs).
- Provide a complete and accurate MLA heading/header (including last name and page number).
- Use present tense, but not first person.
- *Says*, *tells*, and *states* (emphasis added) or variations of these words are not present for the purpose of introducing quotes.
- Do not use contractions: *didn't, can't, don't, won't, he's, she's, they're* (emphasis added), etc..[1]
- The thesis is not a fact; it is a specific argumentative sentence.
- Each source is introduced, quoted, and cited in parenthetical documentation.
- Each supporting paragraph features specific quotes that are required for thesis support.
- Quotes are put into context, and their importance is demonstrated in the sentence in which they are introduced.
- The Works Cited section (last page of your paper) is complete, accurate, and perfectly formatted.

---

1 *MLA Handbook for Writers of Research Papers* (New York: The Modern Language Association of America, 2009), 74.

A

Demonstrates creative and critical thinking

Demonstrates insight: it appears that the writer has discovered something through the act of writing

Demonstrates superior word choice

Offers argumentative analysis via a legitimate and an original thesis

Expertly organized, with meticulously crafted sentences

Few (single-digit) errors

Complete and accurate introduction, quoting, and documentation/citation of all sources

Demonstrates a mastery of MLA format

Near-perfect Works Cited list, which is complete and accurate

Near-perfect introduction of writers and titles (when they are required), quoting, and the introduction of these quotes in a sentence that demonstrates why the quotes are relevant to thesis support

Quotes are expertly introduced, using a variety of words, and put into context in the same sentence, demonstrating why they are vital to thesis support

Supporting paragraphs feature thesis support from multiple sources per paragraph

B

Displays some creativity and independent thought

Offers argumentative analysis via a legitimate thesis

May exhibit grammatical and/or mechanical problems

Double-digit errors

Slightly flawed and incomplete Works Cited list

Few (single-digit) MLA errors

Demonstrates some improvement between first and final drafts

C

Offers a sentence that at the very least can be technically defined as a thesis

Fulfills the assignment with little creative and original thought

Displays factual or interpretative inconsistencies

Contains a general main idea that lacks insight

An inadequate/inaccurate Works Cited section

D

Fails to respond to the demands of the assignment

Significantly confusing or inconsistent concepts and/or interpretations

Vague and veers off topic/loses focus

Repetitive and poor word choices

Simply summarizes without offering any analysis or argument

Excessive errors

Does not exhibit standard written English

F

Plagiarized

Bears no resemblance to an MLA-style critical paper

Ridiculously underdeveloped and incoherent, so much so that the reader is unable to understand

Has no focus and has never been revised

Disciplined and organized writers can be disciplined and organized students and citizens outside of the classroom. Writing is a process that you will master and apply in your personal and professional life. In the age of social media, it is still important to be articulate if you are attempting to persuade someone to hire or promote you. Your skills may make the difference when all other things appear to be equal.

You will find that understanding the fundamental elements of advanced writing can be achieved through practice and diligence.

CREDITS

Fig. P.1: Chief Photographer/MOD, "Operating a Computer Keyboard MOD 45158106," https://commons.wikimedia.org/wiki/File:Operating_a_Computer_Keyboard_MOD_45158106.jpg. Copyright © 2014 by Defence Imagery. Reprinted with permission.

Fig. 1.1: Edward Hopper, "Nighthawks by Edward Hopper 1942," https://commons.wikimedia.org/wiki/File%3ANighthawks_by_Edward_Hopper_1942.jpg. Copyright in the Public Domain.

CPSIA information can be obtained
at www.ICGtesting.com
Printed in the USA
FSHW021352041219
64675FS